CRAFT TOPICS

VIKINGS

FACTS ● THINGS TO MAKE ● ACTIVITIES

RACHEL WRIGHT

FRANKLIN WATTS

LONDON•SYDNEY

© 1992 Franklin Watts
This edition 2001

Franklin Watts
96 Leonard Street
London EC2A 4XD

Franklin Watts Australia
56 O'Riordan Street
Alexandria, Sydney, NSW 2015

ISBN 0 7496 4194 0

Editor: Hazel Poole
Consultant: Dr Dominic Tweddle
Design: Sally Boothroyd
Photography: Chris Fairclough
Artwork: Ed Dovey
Additional picture research: Juliet Duff

A CIP catalogue record for this book is
available from the British Library

Printed in Dubai

CONTENTS

THE VIKINGS ABROAD

RAIDERS . . .

The "Viking Age" began in the late 700s, when ship-loads of warriors left their homes in Scandinavia to plunder the coasts of western Europe. These sea-borne raiders, known as Vikings, wreaked havoc wherever they went. They ransacked churches and monasteries, stole treasure, seized prisoners as slaves, and slaughtered anyone who stood in their way.

. . . SETTLERS

During the 800s, these swift and savage raids became more frequent. They also became more organized. Instead of just smashing and grabbing, the Vikings started to settle in the lands they attacked. By the mid to late 800s, they had colonised parts of England, Ireland and Scotland.

The Vikings were adventurers. They crossed the unknown Atlantic Ocean to lands which few, if any, Europeans had explored.

In about AD 870, a group of Norwegian Vikings settled in Iceland, and in AD 982, Eirik the Red discovered Greenland. Although the land he sighted was icy and desolate in parts, he named it "Green" in the hope that others would be persuaded to settle there.

Twenty years after Eirik's discovery, his son, Leif, became the first European to land in North America. A small number of Vikings then tried to settle in America, but their plan backfired. After they had been there only a few years, they ran into trouble with some native Americans and were forced to head back home.

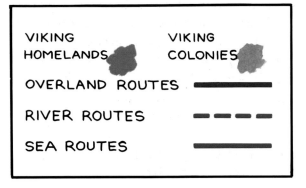

VIKING HOMELANDS	VIKING COLONIES
OVERLAND ROUTES	▬▬▬
RIVER ROUTES	▬ ▬ ▬
SEA ROUTES	▬▬▬

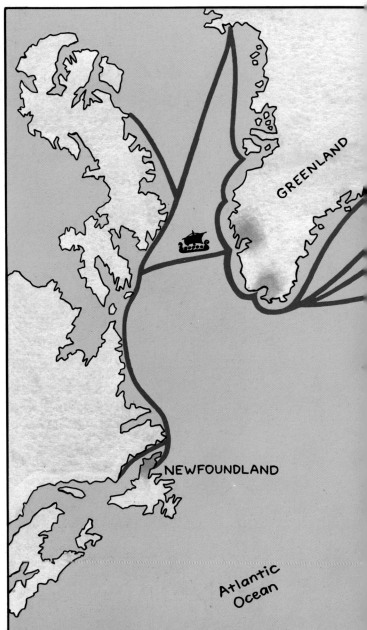

GREENLAND

NEWFOUNDLAND

Atlantic Ocean

... AND TRADERS

Raiding and trading went together, and the Vikings were good at both. They often combined raids with trading expeditions, and sold their stolen goods and prisoners of war at home and abroad.

The Swedish Vikings, in particular, were remarkable traders. They sailed down Russia's main rivers, taking over and setting up trading posts as they went. They even ventured down as far as the Black Sea and Central Asia. In return for slaves and goods from their cold homelands, such as furs, fish, amber, honey and walrus ivory, the Vikings were given silks, spices, silver, wine and glass. These luxury goods were eagerly sought by traders and customers back in Scandinavia.

Viking activity continued in Europe and beyond for nearly 300 years. When it ceased in the late 1000s, the Viking Age came to an end.

▼ *This map shows just how far the Vikings ventured. Although they made their mark wherever they settled, the Vikings were greatly influenced by the people they met.*

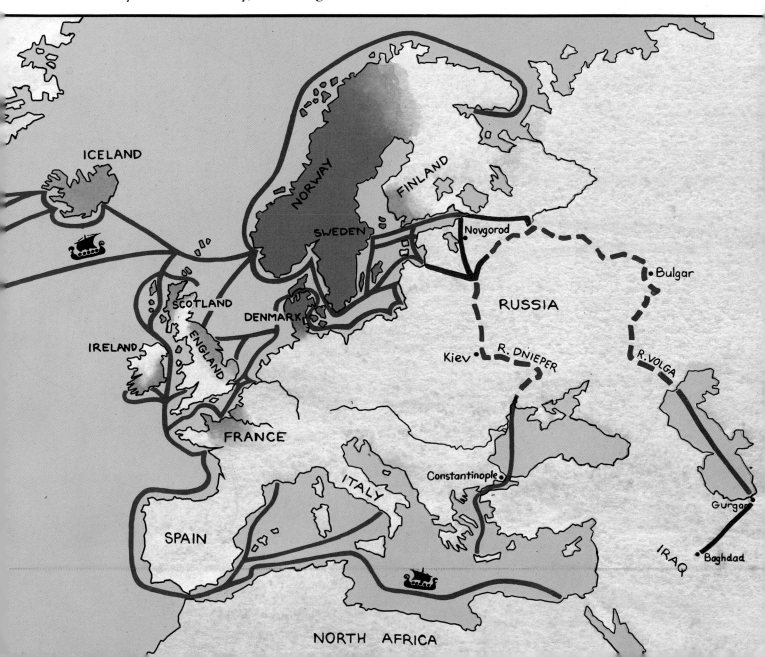

ICELAND

NORWAY

FINLAND

SWEDEN

Novgorod

Bulgar

SCOTLAND

RUSSIA

DENMARK

IRELAND

ENGLAND

Kiev

R. DNIEPER

R. VOLGA

FRANCE

ITALY

Constantinople

Gurgan

SPAIN

IRAQ

Baghdad

NORTH AFRICA

SERPENTS OF THE SEA

One of the reasons why the Viking raids upon western Europe were successful was because the countries under attack were weak and divided, without strong coastal defences. But the main reason for the success of these raids was due to the fact that they were launched from the sea. The Vikings were superb sailors and unrivalled shipbuilders. Their victims simply couldn't match them at sea, which may explain why they never launched revenge attacks on the Vikings' homelands.

THE GOKSTAD SHIP

The Vikings built different kinds of ships for different tasks. For raids they would probably have used a ship like this one found buried at Gokstad in Norway.

The Gokstad ship was built in about AD 800. It is over 23 metres long and about 5 metres wide.

THE MAST AND SAILS

The tall pine mast slotted into blocks of wood attached to the keel. When it was lowered, it probably rested on three T-shaped posts standing in the middle of the ship. In stormy weather the square sail could be taken down from the mast and lowered over the posts, like a tent, to protect the crew.

Like all Viking ships, the Gokstad ship was low which meant that it could sail in fairly shallow water.

The sides were made from long, overlapping wooden planks, nailed together with iron rivets. Animal hair, dipped in tar, was wedged between each plank to make the ship watertight. The planks were thin, which helped to keep the ship light. This made it easier to pull ashore, and helped to make it faster to sail.

OARS

Although Viking longships were sailing vessels, they also had oars. These were probably used in windless weather and for getting in and out of harbour. Oars were also used to row ashore where there were no harbours.

The steering was controlled by a large, heavy oar attached to the back of the ship, on the right-hand side. This combination of sail and oars, together with the shape and flexibility of the hull, made Viking ships faster and more mobile than other European ships.

The sturdy backbone, or keel, was made from the trunk of an oak tree.

NAVIGATION

Whenever possible, the Vikings sailed within sight of land. When they were far out at sea, they used the North star and the Sun to guide them. They could also tell how close they were to land by the numbers and types of birds, driftwood and seaweed they saw.

FIGUREHEADS

The Vikings often carved a ship's prow, or front, with a menacing animal head. They then gave the ship a name to suit its figurehead, such as "Long Serpent" or "Raven of the Sea".

7

BUILD A LONGSHIP

Ask a grown-up to help you as the knife blade will be sharp!

The measurements given here are only a guide. You can make this ship any size you like.

TO MAKE THE "DECK"

1. Cut out a large square of card 30cm x 30cm and draw a diagonal line between two of its corners.

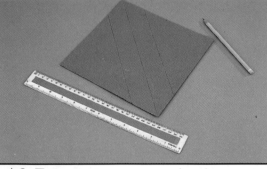

▲2. Turn your square round and draw a line either side of the centre line. Both outer lines should be about 5cm from the centre.

▲3. Using a ruler to guide you, gently run the tip of your craft knife along both outer lines. Fold the lines inwards, to create two triangles, and then cut the top off each triangle.

TO MAKE THE SHIP'S SIDES

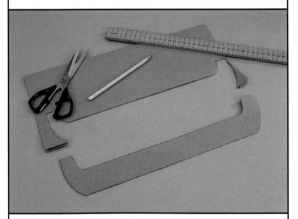

▲4. Cut out a piece of card 55cm x 20cm. Fold the card in half lengthways and draw the side of a ship on it. The bottom edge of your drawing needs to be about 48cm long. When you are happy with the shape of your drawing, cut it out.

TO MAKE OARS

5. Glue paddle-shaped pieces of card onto the ends of cocktail sticks.

Real Viking ship oar holes had slits on one side to push the oar blades through.

TO MAKE OAR HOLES

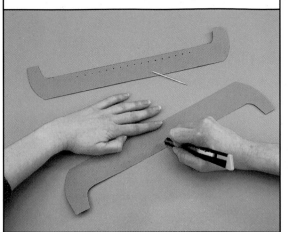

▲6. Use a craft knife to cut a line of tiny crosses along the sides of your ship. Gently push a cocktail stick into the crosses, to open them up.

7. Paint your ship's "deck", sides and oars. When the paint has dried, glue the ship's sides together at the front and back.

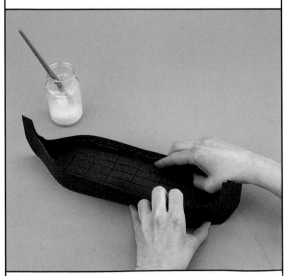

▲8. Spread glue around the edge of the "deck", and stick it about half way up the ship's sides, below the oar holes.

The Vikings used the space between the "deck" and the bottom of the ship for storing spare oars and rope.

TO MAKE THE MAST AND SAIL

9. Roll some stiff paper into two long thin tubes. Hold each of the tubes together with glue and then paint them.

TO MAKE A MAST HOLDER

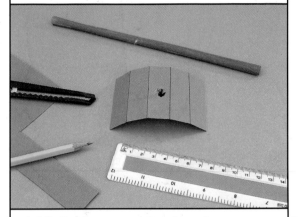

▲10. Fold a rectangle of card, 12.5cm x 5cm, into five equal-sized panels. Make a hole in the middle panel, just big enough for one of the paper tubes to fit into it.

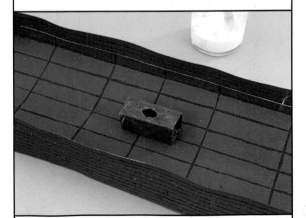

▲11. Glue the two end panels together. Now paint your mast holder and glue it to the centre of the ship's "deck".

12. Using the needle and thread, sew loops along the top of your piece of cloth, and slide one of the paper poles through the loops.

9

▲ 13. Glue or tie the two poles together with thread, and slot the mast and sail into place. If your mast wobbles, wedge some plasticine inside its holder.

TO MAKE AN OARSMAN'S CHEST

▲ 15. Mark and cut a square of card 5cm x 5cm, as shown.

Each oarsman sat on a wooden chest, packed with his belongings.

TO MAKE A FIGUREHEAD

▲ 14. Trace the shape below onto a folded piece of card. Cut it out, paint it and then glue it to your ship's prow. Now push all the oars into place.

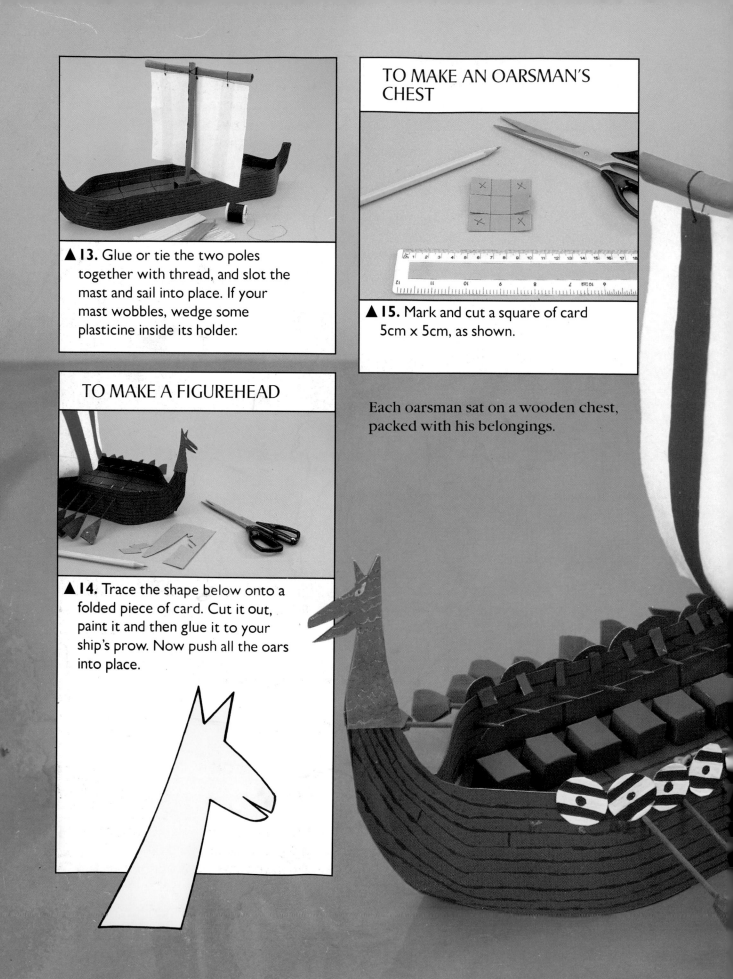

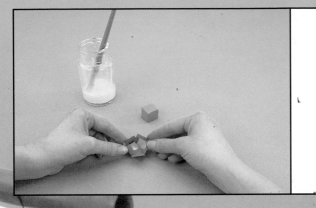

16. Spread some glue on the back of the tabs marked x. Fold them inwards and glue them to their nearest panels, to make a box.

17. Turn the box over, paint it, and glue it next to an oar hole.

When coming into harbour, the Vikings sometimes hung their shields on the side of their ships.

TO MAKE A SHIELD

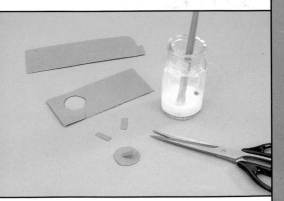

▲**18.** Glue a tiny strip of folded card onto the back of a card circle. When you have made as many shields as you need, paint them and hang them along your ship's sides.

LAW AND ORDER

During most of the Viking Age, Sweden, Norway and Denmark each had their own king and royal family. Although each king was the most important person in his own land, he was only slightly more powerful than his nobles.

The nobles, or jarls as they were called, were warrior aristocrats. They owned land, farms, ships and slaves, and financed raiding and trading expeditions.

The crews for these expeditions were mainly made up of free-born peasants, called karls. Karls were the craftsmen, traders and farmers of the Viking world. Some owned or rented farm land. Others worked on a jarl's farm.

The dirtiest and smelliest jobs on any farm were done by slaves called thralls. Thralls had to work hard for their owners, and sleep in a draughty outbuilding. Unlike the jarls and karls, they had few rights in law.

Large Things were like fairs. People set up camp, chatted, traded, and watched their favourite sports.

SORTING THINGS OUT AT THE "THING"

The Vikings didn't have separate law courts and parliaments as we do today. They settled lawsuits and tried criminals at open air meetings called "Things". Each district would hold a Thing whenever necessary, and all the local jarls and karls would be invited to have their say. When everyone had spoken and a decision had been reached, they all clashed their weapons together to show that they were in agreement.

The Vikings didn't have prisons. Most serious criminals found guilty by the Thing were either fined or banished. Banishment was the most dreaded punishment of all. Family ties were very important to the Vikings, and to be exiled from one's family was a fate worse than death.

13

WRITING IN RUNES

Viking law was not written down. Lawmen had to learn the law by heart and recite it whenever it was needed. In this way the law was passed by word of mouth from one generation to the next.

The Vikings had no pens, paper or books, and very few of them could read or write. Those who could, wrote in runes. Runes were carved onto wood or stone. They were made up of straight lines because these were easier to carve than curved lines. There were 16 runes in the Viking alphabet.

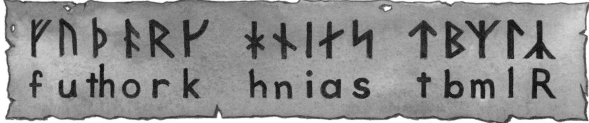

futhork   hnias   tbmlR

This is the runic alphabet. Try using it to write secret messages to your friends, or to carve a name plaque for your bedroom door. If you made the ship on page 8, you could paint its name in runic letters on the prow. (If you need to use a letter not included in the Viking alphabet, invent your own runic version of that letter instead).

▶ *Rune stones were often raised in memory of someone who had died. Some runic inscriptions named the dead person and the man who had erected the stone, and said where the dead person had passed away. Other inscriptions praised the dead person's hospitality, generosity or bravery in battle.*

CLOTHES AND JEWELLERY

Viking men wore long, tight woollen trousers with a pair of linen breeches underneath. They also wore linen or wool shirts with a tunic on top. Rich Viking men sometimes wore shirts made from imported silk and wide, baggy trousers. Only the wealthy could afford to use material in such an extravagant way.

Wealthy Viking women wore long, fine smocks, with sleeveless pinafores over the top. These pinafores were held together with a pair of bronze oval brooches, from which a woman could hang her scissors, needles, knife and keys. These brooches are sometimes called "tortoise" brooches because of their shape.

Both men and women wore leather shoes, and heavy capes to keep them warm outdoors. The men also wore leather or cloth hats. Wealthy married women wore white linen head-dresses and tied their hair back. Only unmarried girls and widows were allowed to wear their hair loose.

The Vikings loved to deck themselves out in gold and silver jewellery. For them, jewellery was a sign of wealth as well as decoration.

15

MAKE SOME VIKING JEWELLERY

You will need: air hardening modelling material/clay • damp sponge • two safety pins • acrylic paint • thin strips of paper • needle and thread • cocktail sticks • glue • clear nail polish • fuse wire • scissors.

Modelling materials sometimes crack when they are being moulded. If this happens, just wipe your hands along a damp sponge and smooth the cracks with your fingers.

TO MAKE A "TORTOISE" BROOCH

1. Roll a piece of modelling material/clay into a smooth round ball.

2. Cup one of your hands and hold the ball in that hand. Straighten the thumb of your other hand and push it into the middle of the ball. Be careful not to push your thumb too far into the clay or else the front of your brooch will be very thin.

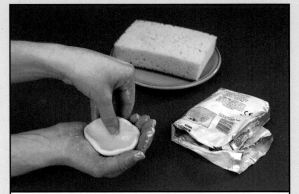

▲ 3. Holding the clay in your cupped hand, gently squeeze its sides with the thumb and fingers of your other hand. Turn the clay as you squeeze it until its sides are of an even thickness.

   Try to carefully stretch the clay into an oval shape as you squeeze and turn.

▲ 4. Roll out a strip of clay, about the same length as your brooch. Flatten one side of the strip and fix it, flat side up, to the back of your brooch. If necessary, dab a bit of water onto the ends of the strip to make it stick.

5. Push a safety pin into this strip and cover its fixed side with a little more clay.

▲ **6.** There are lots of ways you can decorate your brooch. You can press an assortment of objects in it, to give it texture, or you can use a knife to carve the sort of twisting patterns the Vikings loved. You can even plait strands of clay and stick them onto your brooch.

7. When you've finished decorating your brooch, use a cocktail stick to drill a hole in it, near the bottom. Then leave it somewhere warm to dry and make another brooch in the same way.

Viking women often wore necklaces of coloured glass, crystal or amber beads strung between their "tortoise" brooches.

TO MAKE BEADS

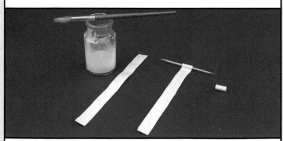

▲ **8.** Brush some glue over one side of a thin strip of paper. Roll the paper around a cocktail stick a couple of times. Then remove the stick and finish rolling the paper by hand.

▲ **9.** To make narrowing beads, cut the strip of paper into a point at one end before gluing and rolling it.

10. Vary the widths of the strips of paper you use, and make lots of beads using both methods. If you want round beads, roll out little balls of clay. Push some fuse wire through each ball, to make a hole.

11. When you have all the beads you need, slide them onto cocktail sticks and paint them. Let the paint dry and then coat them with clear nail polish. When your brooches have dried, paint them too.

12. To finish, thread your beads onto some cotton, and tie the ends of the cotton to the holes in each brooch.

DOWN ON THE FARM

During the Viking Age, most Scandinavians lived in small, isolated farming communities. Crop growing and cattle rearing were their main source of livelihood. However, because much of Scandinavia was covered with forest and mountains, there wasn't a great deal of good farm land to be found.

   To make matters worse, the little suitable land available was often hard to farm because of the harsh, cold Scandinavian climate. This land-shortage problem, together with the problems of overpopulation, may explain why so many Vikings left home in search of new lands.

With farm land in short supply, farmers had to be fishermen and hunters, as well. They killed wild animals, such as deer, boars, bears, whales and seals for food, and used animal skins to make tents and sleeping bags for sea journeys. They also used the animals' bones and antlers to make ice skates, spindles, combs and spoons.

Every farmer's life was ruled by the seasons. In the spring, he would plough his fields with an ox or horse-drawn plough, and plant crops, such as rye, oats and barley. He might then spend the summer raiding overseas, before returning home for the harvest.

WOMEN'S WORK

While the men were away at sea, the women were left in charge of the farms. Their tasks were just as gruelling as their husbands'. They had to milk the cows and goats, make butter and cheese, and prepare all the food. In the autumn, when many of their cattle were killed, the women salted the meat to preserve it. They had to make sure that there was enough food to last through the long cold winter months.

The women weren't only responsible for providing food. They also had to spin sheep's wool and beat flax into thread. The flax was then woven on looms into linen, and the wool was woven into woollen cloth. The women used the cloth to make blankets, wall hangings, clothes and ship sails.

Viking children didn't go to school. Instead they had to help with the chores at home, and learn practical skills. The girls were shown how to cook, sew, skin animals and run a household. The boys were taught to plough, hunt, fish and fight.

Not all Vikings lived in farming communities. Many craftsmen found it more profitable to live in trading towns near the sea.

WARRIORS AND WEAPONS

The Vikings not only battled abroad. They also fought amongst themselves at home. Every Viking male had to learn how to fight. He had to be ready to defend his home, to make a stand in family feuds, and to protect his local jarl's land, if necessary.

No self-respecting free-born Viking ever left home without his favourite weapons – his double-edged iron sword, or his broad-edged battle-axe. He may also have owned a spear and a bow and arrows, which he could use for hunting, as well as fighting.

The Vikings cherished their weapons. They gave them magnificent names and decorated them with precious metals. The blacksmiths who made and repaired many of these iron weapons, as well as all the farm tools, were highly regarded by everyone.

The most important defensive weapons which the Vikings had were their shields. Round, slightly curved and made of wood, each shield had an iron "boss" in the centre to protect its owner's hand. Those who could afford it also wore a coat of iron mail over their clothes, and a leather or metal helmet.

PREPARE FOR BATTLE

Ask a grown-up to help you.

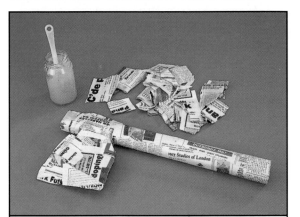

TO MAKE A BATTLE-AXE

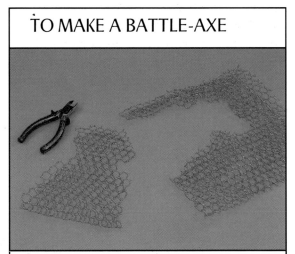

▲ **1.** Fold a rectangle of chicken wire in half and cut out the shape of an axe-head. Don't cut away the fold as this will become the blade of your axe.

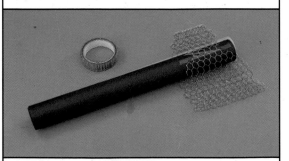

▲ **2.** Roll some stiff paper into a long, thick tube and glue the edge down. Now tape your tube and wire axe-head together, as shown.

▲ **3.** Cover your axe with strips of newspaper coated with wallpaper paste. Let the paper dry thoroughly before adding another layer. Keep adding layers of newspaper until you can no longer feel any bits of wire underneath.

4. The Vikings liked to adorn their weapons and jewellery with swirly animal patterns. When your axe has dried, you can either paint similar patterns with a brush, or glue twirls of painted string on it.

▲ **5.** If your axe-head isn't too bumpy, glue some string around a cardboard tube. Paint the string and, while it's still wet, roll the tube along your axe. This will create a repeating design.

21

TO MAKE A HELMET

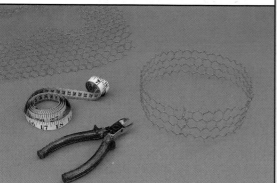

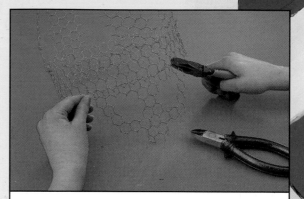

▲6. Measure around your head with a tape measure. Cut a strip of chicken wire about 3 or 4cms longer than your head measurement. Bend this strip into a circle and carefully fasten the two ends together by winding their ragged wire edges around each other.

▲8. Cut out an eye-guard like the one shown here, and attach it to the front of your helmet. You may need to bend the eye-guard forward slightly so that it will fit over your nose.

9. Follow the instructions given in step **3** and cover your helmet, inside and out, with layers of newspaper. Before you paint your helmet, make sure that there are no wire edges sticking out.

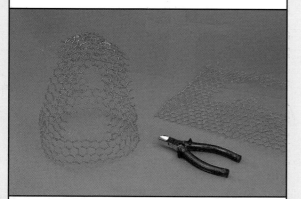

▲7. Cut two more strips of chicken wire. They need to be long enough to reach from one side of the circle, over your head to the other side. Fasten the two wire strips to the circle to form a skeleton helmet.

TO MAKE A SHIELD

▲10. Draw a large circle on a piece of thick card and cut it out. Cut a strip of thick card, long enough to make a handle, and tape it to the back of your shield, just above the middle.

11. Cover your shield with a couple of layers of pasted newspaper to strengthen it.

▲12. To make a boss for your shield, mould small sheets of pasted newspaper into a mound. Glue this paper mound to the front of the shield, in the middle.

When your shield has dried, paint it. Then put on your helmet, grab your axe and get ready to raid!

Viking houses were made from whatever kind of building material was most readily available. Some were built of posts, with a mixture of straw and clay plastered between the posts. Others had plank walls, or turf walls lined with wood. In treeless regions, stone, clay and turf were used instead of wood.

INSIDE A LONG-HOUSE

A jarl and his family often lived in their farm's main building, called the long-house. Long-houses were like gloomy hallways with an open fire in the middle of the floor. They were always smoky because there were few, if any, windows, and only a small hole in the roof to let out the fire's smoke.

Many long-houses were like a living room, dining room, bedroom and kitchen, all rolled into one. They were cramped and uncomfortable, without carpets or sofas to lounge about on. The earthen floors were strewn with reeds, and the benches that lined the walls served as beds at night.

Wealthy Vikings had tables and chairs, but no-one had cupboards. Everyone stored their belongings in wooden chests instead. At mealtimes the Vikings used plates, knives and spoons, but not forks. They drank beer, mead and sometimes wine from wooden cups or glasses. They also drank from cowhorns, which were passed from drinker to drinker.

FEASTS AND FESTIVALS

The high spots of the Viking year were the three major festivals or feasts. The first of these feasts was held after Christmas and animal sacrifices were offered to the gods to ensure good crops in the spring. The second feast was held in April, and sacrifices were offered for victory in the summer raids. The third feast was held after the harvest, to ask the gods for a mild winter.

Feasts were a good excuse to eat a lot and get very, very drunk, so the Vikings held them whenever they had something to celebrate. After the eating had ended, travelling poets and storytellers would thrill everyone with tales of bloody battles and daring deeds. Storytellers, or skalds as they were called, were always made welcome. They wandered from place to place, reciting sagas and passing on the latest news.

Most houses had roofs made out of reeds, turf or wooden shingles.

turf

The benches that lined the walls of a longhouse were sometimes made of mounds of earth.

RELIGION AND RITUALS

Until they became Christians, the Vikings worshipped many different gods.

Their most powerful god was Odin, the god of war. Ferocious and terrifying, Odin thirsted for knowledge. Every day his two ravens, Huginn (Thought) and Muninn (Memory), would fly around the world and report back to him.

Odin was also the god of poets and dead warriors. Vikings who died bravely in battle were expected to go to Odin's heaven, called Valhalla. There they would be free to fight all day and feast all night.

Thor was the favourite god of the karls. They called upon him whenever they were in trouble. They also wore his symbol – the mighty hammer – around their necks, to keep away evil spirits.

Thor was the god of thunder, lightning, wind and rain. The Vikings believed that whenever he raced across the clouds in his goat-drawn chariot, thunder crashed and lightning cracked.

Frey was the god of nature. Sacrifices were made to him to ensure that the crops grew, the sun shone and all was peaceful. His sister, Freyja, was the goddess of love and dead women. Slain warriors who didn't go to Odin's Valhalla joined the dead women in Freyja's fortress.

BURYING THE DEAD

If the spirits of dead warriors and women joined the gods, where did everyone else go after they died? The Vikings didn't have one clear idea about what happened after death. This may explain why they had so many different burial customs. Sometimes they burned their dead. At other times they put the corpse in a large wooden chamber, and either buried it beneath a field or covered it with a mound of earth.

Wealthy warriors were often laid out in ships, which were then buried. Occasionally these burial ships were set alight and pushed out to sea. If an expensive boat couldn't be spared, the corpse was buried in the ground and surrounded by stones arranged in the shape of a boat. Needless to say, poor people were not buried with such ceremony. They were usually just put into a hole in the ground.

The Vikings often buried their loved ones with their most valuable and useful belongings. Perhaps they thought that the dead person would need these earthly possessions in the next world.

THE END OF THE VIKING AGE

It was partly because the Vikings' religion was not well organised that it gave way to Christianity. Although the missionaries who went to Scandinavia were often expelled, they did eventually manage to persuade the Vikings to become Christians.

Christianity changed the Vikings' way of life. They stopped raiding and slave trading, and settled down to peaceful pursuits such as farming and general trading. Many Viking settlers also started to become part of the Christian communities they had invaded. They married the local people, learnt their language and customs, and lost touch with their Scandinavian friends back home.

The Vikings also stopped raiding because the countries they had conquered became much more powerful. These countries gathered together strong armies, capable of resisting attack and driving the Vikings out.

By the late 1000s, the Vikings found that they could no longer ravage and rule Europe as they once had done. The Viking Age had come to an end.

This wooden church was built in Norway in about AD 1150. It has both Christian crosses and pagan dragonheads on its roof.

28

DID YOU KNOW

Contrary to popular belief, the Vikings did not fight in winged or horned helmets. Helmets of this type would have been extremely dangerous, After all, with one swing of his head, a helmet-wearer could easily poke out a comrade's eye.

The Vikings only had a first name, such as Eirik or Harald. So, to distinguish one Eirik or Harald from another, they gave each other nicknames for surnames. The poet, Audun the Bad Bard was so called because he stole some lines from another poet. Eirik the Red was so called because he had red hair. Juice-head may well have had very bad acne!

   A lot of Viking men were named after their fathers. The full name of Eirik the Red's son, Leif, was Leif Eiriksson. Leif's daughter would have been called Leifssdottir.

The most fierce and ferocious Viking warriors of all were called berserkers. Berserkers wore no armour and seemed to feel no pain. In the heat of battle, they would foam at the mouth, bite the rims of their shields in rage, and fight like crazed dogs. Today we use the expression "to go berserk" to describe someone in a frenzy.

No one is sure where the word "Viking" comes from. Some scholars think that it may come from the Norse word "vik", meaning "a bay". As one expert has pointed out "a Viking was a pirate who lay hidden in a fjord, creek or bay, waiting to pounce on passing vessels".*
   Another theory suggests that the word comes from the Norse word "vikja", meaning "to move away from home".

*Quote taken from The Vikings by Johannes Brønsted, first published by Penguin in 1960.

GLOSSARY

Bard – another word for a poet.

Cattle – animals that eat grass such as oxen, cows, sheep and horses.

Colonise – to form a settlement, or colony, in a foreign country.

Figurehead – a carved figure on the front of a ship.

Fjord – a long narrow inlet of sea water, lined on either side by steep cliffs. Norway's coastline has many fjords.

Flax – a stringy plant used to make linen.

Hull – the body or frame of a ship.

Keel – the lowest part of a ship, running along the bottom from prow to stern. A keel helps to keep a ship stable.

Lawsuit – an argument or problem brought before a court of law.

Mead – an alcoholic drink made from honey.

Missionary – someone who is sent to convert others to their own religious faith.

Norse – the language of the ancient Scandinavians, or Vikings.

Prow – the front end of a ship. The back part is called the stern.

Saga – an action-packed story about Viking gods and heroes. At first, the sagas were learnt and told by skalds (storytellers), who passed them on by word of mouth. It was only after the Viking Age had ended that a learned Icelander wrote these sagas down.

Scandinavia – the name given to Norway, Denmark, Sweden and Iceland.

Spindle – a pin used to twist wool into thread.

RESOURCES

BOOKS TO READ

The Time Traveller Book of Viking Raiders by A. Civardi and J. Graham Campbell. (Usborne).

History Highlights – Viking Longboats by M. Mulvihill. (Franklin Watts).

The Ancient World – The Vikings by P. Odijk. (Macmillan).

I Was There – Vikings by John D. Clare. (Bodley Head).

Fiction

Usborne Illustrated Guide to Norse Myths and Legends by C. Evans and A. Millard.

The Saga of Eric the Viking by Terry Jones. (Puffin).

There's a Viking in My Bed by Jeremy Strong. (A & C Black).

PLACES TO VISIT

Jorvik Viking Centre
Coppergate
York
YO1 1NT
Tel: (0904) 643211

Opening Times: 1st April until 1st October: 0900-1900. From 1st November until 31st March: 0900-1730.

Jorvik is a carefully reconstructed Viking city. A time-car journey gives visitors the chance to experience the sight, sounds and smells of Viking Age York.

The ARC
(Archaeological Resource Centre)
St Savioursgate
York
YO1 1NT
Tel: (0904) 654324

Opening Times: 1st April until 31st October: Mon-Fri 1000-1700. Sat & Sun 1300-1700. (Closed Good Friday). November, February and March: Mon-Fri 1000-1700.

The ARC is an award-winning hands-on exploration for all the family. Visitors can handle Viking finds, learn Viking skills and meet archaeologists.
   There are special exhibitions and children activity mornings throughout the year, too.

There are various museums throughout the British Isles with collections of Viking objects. These are a few of them –

The Yorkshire Museum
Museums Gardens
York
Tel: (0904) 629 745

The British Museum,
Great Russell Street,
London
WC1B 3DG
Tel: 071-636 1555-8.

The National Museum of Ireland,
Dublin.

On the last Tuesday in January, the people of Lerwick, in the Shetland Islands, celebrate their Viking ancestry with a festival called Up-Helly-Aa. The festivities include the burning of a replica Viking ship.

Index

Additional photographs: Michael Holford 16, 20(bm); University Museum of National Antiquities, Oslo, Norway 6, 7 (Eirik Irgens Johnsen); Werner Forman Archive 14, 20(bl), 20(tl), 20(tr), 28; York Archaeological Trust 20(br).